Hiring Resumes Presents...

Interview Presentation - A "How to" Guide for Job Seekers

"Helping you today...Be prepared for TOMORROW!"

Copyright © 2007 Shenya Brooks.   All rights reserved.
ISBN 978-1-257-84288-9

Dedication

To the heavenly father, thank you for blessing me, for guiding me, and for loving me unconditionally. I know none of this would be possible without you! Thank you for ALWAYS being there for me, and for never leaving my side.

To my children and the love of my life that God has blessed me with. Thank you for believing in me, and showing me your love and support. Thank you for being there for me from start to finish, for better or for worst, and staying with me until the end.

In loving memory of my mother who is always in my heart. Who looks down from heaven above and smiles saying "Well done!" I love and miss you everyday!

To my family and friends thank you for being there whenever I needed you.

I love each and every one of you!

God Bless!

Remember:

What is meant to make us weak will only make us STRONG!

Table of Contents

I. Introduction
- i. Hiring Resumes 5

II. Getting Ready for Work
- i. Seeking Employment 6
- ii. Career and Job Fair 9
- iii. What is a Cover Letter? 10
- iv. Why a Professional Resume? 13
- v. What Employers Expect from Future Employees 16

III. The Key to Success
- i. Presentation is Everything! 18
- ii. Dressing for Success 20

IV. Interviewing
- i. The Different Styles of Interviewing 23
- ii. Interview Tips 24
- iii. Interviewing Exercise 27
- iv. Interview Do's and Don'ts 38

V. Frequently Asked Questions 45

I. Introduction

Hiring Resumes

Hiring Resumes is a professional resume consultant company that specializes in creating as well as re-constructing resume's and career portfolios for job seekers. Our consultants also coach and train individuals on how to interview with confidence with our Interview Preparation Course.

Hiring Resumes Presents….Interview Presentation A "How to" Guide for Job Seekers was written by some of the finest Human Resources Representatives, Hiring Managers, and Recruiters in the world. They know what employers look for in potential candidates, and future employees. Their qualifications as well as having the experience of working with some of the world's top companies and corporation has made them experts in the field of interviewing .

This guide is designed to teach job seekers how to interview with self-assurance. You will learn how to look, dress, and play the part of a professional as well as have a "Go Get It" attitude when interviewing. This guide is also filled with ***Interviewing Tips, Resume Presentation, Dressing for Success, Interviewing Exercise, and More!!!***

Hiring Resumes believe a person can do anything he/she set their minds to doing. In order to be successful in life you have to want it bad enough to succeed. This guide is one of the keys to helping you unlock the many doors of success.

II. Getting Ready for Work

Some job seekers find it hard to choose the right employer because they don't know what steps to take when choosing the correct company they wish to work for.

Seeking Employment

When seeking employment, look for a job that is right for you. Be certain that your skills, and work experience is equivalent to the qualifications for the job. Many job seekers make the mistake of taking a job because they need one, but it's not the job they actually want. You don't want a job to be just a job, but one you can make a career out of. Here are some steps you should take when looking for employment;

1. Go for what you know, and look for a job that you will love, have a desire for, and the passion to perform the work. You want to enjoy where you work, what you do, and know it is more then just a paycheck.

2. Before you apply for any job; make certain the company is a company you can see yourself working for, and growing with. Go to the company's website, and look under "About Us" to find out more information on that company. Research them to see how they operate, and ask yourself some of these questions; What direction is the company taking going toward the future? Where is the company's market growth? What benefits do they offer their

employees? Where do I see myself in this company? Do they offer employee training, and encourage career growth? How do they treat their employees? By asking yourself these questions you determine if the company is a good company, and if it is the right one for you.

3. Don't apply for a job that you do not have the skills for. Read the qualifications needed for the position, and match those qualifications to your skills.

4. Location, location, location! Sometimes, we don't realize how bad traffic could be until we are actually in it. Map your destination to determine how far you will have to travel to and from work, and decide if that is the job for you.

5. Salary is very important when seeking employment, and knowing what you're worth is just as important. Base your salary on how many years of experience you have, and what you feel you should be paid. If you are not sure on how much you should be paid, go to an employment salary website. There you can put in your information, and the salary wizard or calculator can give you an estimate of what you're worth, and where you should be salary wise.

6. Education is one of the key factors employers look for in potential candidates. Not only do they want to make sure you have the skills to perform the job, they also want to make sure you have the knowledge to do the job as well. Don't let this be a discouragement

for you. Some employers will still look at a resume of a potential candidate, and determine if the years of experience is equivalent *(equal)* to the educational level and years of experience required to be eligible for the position. Example: If the position requires a Bachelors' degree along with four (4) years of experience to qualify; you will need a total of eight (8) years of experience to be considered equivalent for the job. The trick is to add the educational years with the years of experience required to get the equivalent number of years needed for the position.

Below are some educational levels and their translations in years that employers use to qualify potential candidates. The employer determines if the years of experience is equivalent to the education level, and the years of experience needed to meet the criteria for the position.

- Associate's Degree – Two (2) years of school or work related experience.
- Bachelors' Degree – Four (4) years of school or work related experience.
- Master's Degree – Eight (8) years of school or work related experience.
- Doctorate / PhD – Ten (10) years of school or work related experience.

This is to help you when applying for a job, so you will know how many years of experience you need without the education plus the years of experience needed to be consider for the position. *(Remember to*

ADD *the two together.).* If you keep these steps in mind, you will find that dream job you always wanted with the company you always dreamed about.

Career and Job Fairs

We see advertisement for career and job fairs everyday rather it's on the television, the radio, on the internet, in the Sunday newspaper or on a billboard sign; we see them. A career fair is the same thing as a job fair. They are events where local and out of state companies and corporations come together, and search for new talent. This event is a job seekers dream! It is a wonderful opportunity for job seekers to pass out their resumes, and be discovered by the hiring company.

When going to a career or job fair; take the time to look around, and see what companies and corporations are present. With an event like this, you want to decide which company or companies are the best ones for you; where you can utilize your skills and talents. The most important thing to remember is to treat the career or job fair as if it's an actual job interview. You must walk the walk and talk the talk as well as look and act the part of a professional. Your appearance as well as your professionalism will be looked upon from the time you walk through the doors to the time you come, and talk to one of the company representatives.

Employers who are a part of this event send their BEST agents to find outstanding talent to represent the company, so you always want to make a good impression that will be a lasting impression. If you want to get the job make sure you;

1. Look and act like a professional.
2. Have a clean and professional copy of your resume.
3. Ask questions about the company and what they do.

Remembering these things may help you get notice, maybe an actual interview with the company, and maybe get the job!

What is a Cover Letter?

A cover letter is a letter that is sent with your resume when applying for a job. It is a formal introduction of who you are to the employer, and gives a brief outline of the position you are inquiring about as well as your skills when applying for the job. A cover letter is the opening act to get the employer's attention to view your resume, and should always be used when you are applying for a position. Your cover letter should be clean, readable, well written, and professional from beginning to end.

Make sure your cover letter displays the skills or experiences that are required to meet the criteria for the job. You want to get the employers attention so he/she will want to look at your resume to view your other skills and talents, and maybe consider you for the open position. Most employers wouldn't even look at a resume without a cover letter. Sending your resume without a cover letter will have the employer confuse and wondering what position you are inquiring about, and your resume may become trash.

If you want a position that will allow you to utilize your skills then make sure the employer knows this in your cover letter because if you don't, the employer will put you in a position that you will not be happy with. Your cover letter and resume are tools to help you get notice, get the interview, and get the job! See page 12 for an example of a cover letter.

Address
City, State, Zip Code
Telephone:
Mobile:
Email:

Date

Company Name
Attention: Hiring Manager
Company Address
City, State, Zip
Ref/Position:

Dear Sir or Madam:

I am inquiring about the position/s that is or may be available at **(Company Name)**. Currently, I am employed with Company 1 – Norcross, GA as an IT Coordinator.

As an IT Coordinator, my responsibilities include but are not limited to:

- Perform typical hardware replacement and installation for devices such as hard drives, memory, CD-ROM, NIC cards and internal modems.
- Support Desktop/LAN services involving multiple Operating Systems (OS) and LAN-based groupware packages or E-mail system.

As a skillful professional in the technology industry with solid communication skills (written and oral) as well as creative and analytical skills has given me the ability to develop, and implement new ideas as well as work collaboratively with others from different cultural and educational backgrounds.

Being a self-starter, team player, and fast learner has made me a valuable asset at Company 1. If given the opportunity I know will be a valuable asset within your organization as well.

Attached/Enclosed is a copy of my resumes showing my talents and expertise's, and I look forward to hearing from you soon.

Sincerely,
John Doe
Attachment/Enclosure

Why a Professional Resume?

A Professional Resume is an outline of your employment history. It tells a story about your career goals, skills, work experiences, educational level, etc.. Your resume should show **EVERYTHING** from your talents and qualifications to your job duties, and responsibilities.

If you are not sure what a professional resume should look like then seek the help of a professional resume writer. They will be able to show you what is wrong, and what needs to be fixed in order to have an outstanding resume. Having a professional resume done for you is the best way to go. Professional resume writers will know how to format your resume, and make it pleasing to the eyes.

How you present yourself on your resume is how the employer will see you. Presenting yourself on paper is like throwing a fabulous dinner party! You pull out all the good stuff; the fine china, the good silverware, the silk linen tablecloth, the pretty stemware, etc. making everything FABULOUS for the big event. Think of your dinner party as your interview, and the fine china is your work experience / employment history you put on your resume; and the silk linen tablecloth is the paper you use to put the fine china (your information) on.

Treat your resume like you would your party. If you know you would never serve your guest dinner on a paper or plastic plate then why would you present your resume on BAD, COPIER or COLOR

PAPER? Use **RESUME PAPER!** Your resume represents you, and who you are. It should be clean, clear, and easy to read.

Your presentation is what makes people talk about you to others, and you always want what they say to be something good and not bad. See page 15 for an example of a professional resume.

John Doe

Address
City, State, Zip Code

Telephone:
Mobile:
Email:

Summary

A professional IT Coordinator with 10 years of experience in the technology industry who has a very strong background in Desktop Administration, Field Service, Customer Relations, Help Desk Support, Troubleshooting, Service Research, Development, System Design, Hardware and Software Installation.

Skills

Operating System
Windows 3.0 & 9X.Windows 95'- 2000', Windows NT, Windows XP.

Hardware
Dell desktop workstations and laptops, HP Vectras, HP Pavilions, IBM desktop workstations and laptop,

Software
MS Office 3.X ~ 2003, WordPerfect 3.x ~10.x, Lotus SmartSuite, Lotus Notes 5.0 & 6.5.4, Lotus Organizer, WinFax, PC Anywhere, ProComm Plus, MS Access, MS Project, MS Publisher, IBM Client Access,

Internet
MS Internet Explorer, Netscape, AOL, MSN.

History of Expertise

Company 1 – Norcross, GA   2006 - Present
Coordinator
- Maintain primary and back-up domain and file sever for the southern regional part of Georgia.

Company 2, Atlanta, GA   2003 - 2006
Network Service Technician III
- Assisted all end users with general computer operation and desktop application software questions and problems.

Education

Gwinnett Technical Institute, Atlanta, GA   1999
Major: Computer Installation and Maintenance

Reference

Available Upon Request

What Employers Expect from Future Employees

Employers want employees who have the knowledge, and know how as well as the skills to do the job. They expect future employees to be truthful, professional, skillful, self-starters, team players, hard working, punctual, ready to work, independent, and proactive with the ability to work in a business environment as well as provide excellent representation of the company.

They want employees who has a "Go Get It" attitude, and who is always willing to go that extra mile to get the job done. That means the employee goes above and beyond the call of duty. They work long hours, stay late, and do what ever it takes to complete the job. Employers want employees who will represent the company the way it should be by being professional from start to finish. Being a team player is also very important to an employer. Employers believe if everyone does their part, and play the role they were given the company will be successful. Knowing that there is no "I" in "Team" will make you successful within the company as well.

Employers do not want employees who are lazy, untruthful, selfish, unskilled, self-centered, unfriendly, complainers, unprofessional, and cannot work in a team environment. They also do not want employees who are late, never ready to work, always blaming others, and never taking the responsibility for their own actions.

Recent studies conducted by over 400 major companies showed high school, and college graduates did have the ability to adept in the workplace or the skills needed to do the job. They were not professional enough, and did not work well within a team setting. They lack leadership and problem solving skills, and was unable to communicate effectively (verbally or written) in a business environment. Employers believe to have an effective workforce; high school and college graduates must be well skilled for entry level position. They must have basic academic and life skills in order to be success in the workplace and in the future.

Understand that employers insist on running a strong and successful business. They need people who are serious about their work, what they do, and what the company stands for. Try to keep these things in mind when looking for employment.

III. The Key to Success

"The key to success is what you make it, and having the right key can help you open many doors!"

<u>Presentation is Everything</u>

When employers hire for open position they look for these key elements in potential candidates;

1. Skills & Knowledge. You must know the job inside and out, and the employer will make certain you do. Your skills, and knowledge are tested from the time your resume is reviewed to the time you come in, and interview face to face.

2. Positive Attitude & Confidence. When being interviewed you must talk the talk, and walk the walk. Let the interviewer/s see what you are made of with confidence and not arrogance. Knowing the difference between the two is very important. Here's a hint; CONFIDENCE is respected and ARROGANCE is rejected!

3. Presentation. First impressions are lasting impressions, and how you present yourself to an employer says a lot. You must be professional from the time you get there to the time you leave. Remember: Presentation is everything, and it is also the key to success.

4. Appearance. Dress for success! You must look and play the part of a professional at all times before, during, and after an interview. "Before" is when you are waiting to be seen, "During" is when you are in the interview, and "After" when you leave.

5. Personality. Your personality should be polite, respectable, and friendly. Employers not only look at your skills, but they look at how you interact with them during the interview. Your personality tells a lot about you, and how you will fit in with the other employees in their company.

6. Professionalism. Your professionalism will tell an employer how professional you really are. How you represent yourself will show the employer how you will represent their company from beginning to end.

Remembering these key elements will help you achieve those goals that will make you successful in the job market.

Dressing for Success

You heard it before, and I'll say it again…"First impressions are lasting impressions!" How you present yourself in an interview to an employer is how he or she will see you throughout the entire interview. When going to an interview there are some important things you should **ALWAYS** remember;

1. **ALWAYS** wear a SUIT! A Blue, Black or Gray suit should be worn regardless of the employment industry you are being interviewed for. Your suit should fit you properly, and should not be baggy looking. The cuffs on your suit jacket sleeve should come to your wrist, and the hem of your trousers (pants) should come right below the ankle bone. Men should wear a white shirt, and a solid color or nicely printed tie with their suit. Women should wear a white or cream color blouse (with or without a collar, but not a v-neck) with their suit, and hosieries (pantyhose) if wearing a skirt or trouser socks/socking if wearing trousers (pants).

2. **ALWAYS** carry a business portfolio or brief case. Also, bring clean copies of your resume with you. It looks professional, and your resume may be requested by the interviewer/s during the interview.

3. **ALWAYS** be well groomed from top to bottom. Looking the part of a professional will show the employer that you are serious about your job as well as your appearance.

4. **ALWAYS** keep it simple. If wearing jewelry, try to wear as little as possible. Women should wear small earrings, and a watch. Men should wear a watch.

The idea is to **ALWAYS** look professional. It is important to let your appearance be just as pleasing as your personality. See page 22 for an example on how you should dress when going to an interview.

REMEMBER TO KEEP IT NEAT & SIMPLE!!!

VI. Interviewing

An interview is the employer's way of searching for talent. They want the Superstars, the Best of the Best, and the Einstein of their industry to represent their company. Your resume will go through several viewings, and pre-screenings by the employer before the first call is made.

The Different Styles of Interviewing

There are several styles of interviewing used by employers to help them determine if you would be a good fit for the company or not. Below are some of the most common styles of interviewing;

1. Telephone Interview – This style of interviewing is done over the telephone. It is to test your skills and knowledge as well as to determine if you would be a good fit for the open position within their company. This is also the first step that some employers take before they actually bring you in for a face-to-face interview.

2. One-on-One Interview – This style of interviewing is done face-to-face with one (1) person at a time. It is to test your personal skills as well as your qualification to perform the job. Sometimes, you could interview with as many as five (5) people in one day.

3. Panel Interview – This style of interviewing is also done face-to-face with two (2) or more people. It is to test your professional and people skills, your knowledge and understanding of the job as well as your performance and presentation.

4. Multiple Interview – This style of interviewing is done in person and over the telephone with different interviewers. It is to test ALL of your skills, and to determine where the company can use you and your talents within their organization.

5. Assessment Test Interview – This style of interviewing is done on paper or by email. The employer will send you a set of questions associated to the position you are interviewing for or have interviewed for. It is to test how you think, and how you would handle certain job related situation.

6. Formation Interview - This style of interviewing is done to see if you are truthful about your skills. Each interviewer/s will ask you the same set of questions; this is done to see if your answers are in "formation" with the answers you gave to the other interviewers.

Please understand that notes will be taken during the interview. Everything you say will be written down, and evaluated by the interviewer/s. When the interviews are over, the interviewer/s will get together and compare notes. They will determine if you are the right person to do the job as well the person for their organization.

Interviewing Tips

Here are some helpful tips to assist you when preparing for an interview;

- Study the company you are going to interview with. The more you know about the company, and what they do the better your chances are of getting the job.

- ALWAYS be on TIME! Arrive at least 15 – 20 minutes before your interview starts. You may have to fill out paperwork and/or forms or even take a test before you are seen by the interviewer/s.

- Bring clean copies of your resume. It might be requested by the interviewer/s who may not have a copy on hand. It can also be useful when filling out the application as well. ***Remember your resume is like a fabulous dinner party!***

- Make sure your appearance is neat and professional looking.

- Be polite and respectable from the time you arrive until the time you leave. You will be judged by everyone you meet from the front desk receptionist or greeter to the interviewer/s.

- When greeted; smile and shake hands with the interviewer/s, and introduce yourself again. Example: ***"Hi, Jane Doe."*** This helps the interviewer/s pronounce your name correctly if it is a difficult name to pronounce.

- Never let them see you sweat! Always stay calm during an interview. If you find yourself getting nervous, take short deep breath. Slowly inhale and exhale to help relax your nerves during the interview.

- Make eye contact and speak clearly when answering questions.

- Ask questions! This shows you are interested in the company, and not just looking for a paycheck. Also, ask if it is okay to take notes when asking the questions.

- When the interview is over, remember to shake hands with everyone again. Ask if they have business cards as you hand out your own personal business cards. If they do not have any cards on hand, write down their names. This way you will remember them, and they will remember you.

- Send a "thank you" card/s or letter/s to each interviewer/s. Writing a personal note shows your appreciation for being interviewed.

- Call the interviewer/s or recruiter a week later if you have not heard anything from him or her. This will show you are still interested in the position as well as help you get some feedback about your interview.

If you follow these tips you can have a winning interview.

Interviewing Exercise

In this section you will learn how to answer interview questions. This exercise is to help you become more comfortable as well as gain confidence when being interviewed. Answer each question as if you were in an actual interview. Also, have some fun and practice with a friend. Practice makes perfect!!

1. How are you today?

   _____
   _____

2. Would you like something to drink?

   _____
   _____

3. Tell me a little bit about yourself?

   _____
   _____
   _____
   _____
   _____

4. Where do you see yourself in the next 5 – 10 years?

   _____

   _____

   _____

   _____

   _____

   _____

5. Tell me about your current and/or pervious work experience?

   _____

   _____

   _____

   _____

   _____

   _____

6. Why are you currently looking for a new job?

   _____

   _____

   _____

   _____

   _____

   _____

7. How did you hear about us and/or this position?

   _____

   _____

   _____

   _____

   _____

   _____

8. Why do you think you are a good candidate for this position?

   _____

   _____

   _____

   _____

9. How well do you work with others?

10. Which one of these would you prefer; to work within a group or independently?

11. What are some of your strengths?

_____

_____

_____

_____

_____

12. What are some of your weaknesses?

_____

_____

_____

_____

_____

13. How well do you work under pressure and/or stress?

_____

_____

_____

_____

14. Give an example of how you would handle a situation that involves a co-worker / team member who was not doing their share of the work.

15. How easy is it for you to learn new skills or techniques (ex. Software, Databases, Computer Programs, etc.) related to your job?

16. How well do you work in a fast pace environment?

_____
_____
_____
_____
_____
_____

17. How would you handle a last minute task with a 24 hour deadline?

_____
_____
_____
_____
_____
_____

18. Are you open to working a flexible schedule? If so, what is your availability?

_____
_____
_____
_____

_____

_____

19. What are some of your career goals?

_____

_____

_____

_____

_____

20. Do you have any job related certificate or certifications?

_____

_____

_____

_____

_____

21. What are some of your biggest accomplishments?

_____

_____

22. What were some of your biggest disappointments, and how did you handle it?

23. Which of your skills do you think would be useful within our company?

24. Have you had any job related training? If so, what type of training have you had?

_____
_____
_____
_____
_____

25. Where do you see yourself within our company?

_____
_____
_____
_____
_____

26. What are your salary expectations?

_____
_____
_____

_____

_____

27. Do you have any questions? *(Note – **Write your questions down on a separate piece of paper.**)*

_____

_____

_____

Being prepared for your interview will help you get through it with flying colors!

Interview Do's and Don'ts

There are several Do's and Don'ts that can make or break you in an interview. These rules determine if you are a "Yes" or "No" to receiving the job and working for that company. Below are some do's and don'ts you should think about before you go to an interview.

1. **Do** – Dress for Success! Always look the part of a professional and wear a SUIT! Everyone should own one good blue, black or gray interviewing suit in their closet, and it should fit properly. You should be looking professional from head to toe or should I say from your hair, to your face, to your clothing, to your shoes.
   Don't – Show up to an interview wearing something you would wear to the mall or a night on the town with friends. You should never show up to an interview wearing a suit that is two sizes too big or too small. And when it comes to footwear; you should never come in wearing sandals, open toe shoes, sling back (open heel) shoes, no hosieries (pantyhose), dirty or beat-up looking shoes. This is unprofessional, and can make you lose out on the job. Remember: Presentation is everything!

2. **Do** – Show up on time. Arrive 15 – 20 minutes before the interview actually starts incase you have to fill out paperwork.
   Don't – Be late for an interview. This shows the interviewer/s you are not serious about the job. If you are going to be late, call to inform the interviewer/s, the person who scheduled the interview or the main switchboard of your late arrival.

3. **Do** – Call the day before your interview to confirm the date and time. This shows that you are still interested in the position as well as making sure no changes have been made without your knowledge. Sometime the interviewer/s will change the interview date and/or time, and not inform the candidate.

   Don't – Cancel an interview without informing the company you are interviewing with. If you need to cancel for any reason, call and let the interviewer/s or the person who scheduled the interview know. This can help your chances of receiving another interview with the company if you and/or they are still interested.

4. **Do** – Know your work history. It is very important for you to know what you do and/or did so you can talk about it in the interview. If you know you have had several jobs, and it is hard to remember then study your resume!

   Don't – Pull your resume out during an interview. This looks unprofessional, and it makes you look untruthful. The interviewer/s will question your creditability as well as your skills and qualification to do the job.

5. **Do** – Research the company before you interview. This will help you know important facts about their organization, and the directions they are taking the company in the future. Also, you won't have to worry about being stuck with a company that you are not happy with.

Don't – Pretend to know about the company. Be honest if you don't know, so when a question is asked about the company you won't give the wrong answer.

6. **Do** – Answer each interview question truthfully. Know your skills, your strengths, and your weaknesses for performing the job. Remember you are being tested from the time you get there to the time you leave.

   Don't – Make up or be deceitful about skills you do not have. The interviewer/s are professionals, and they are highly skilled in what they do. So they will know if you got what it takes to do the job, plus it will make you look really bad.

7. **Do** – Speak calmly and clearly. This helps the interviewer/s understand what you are saying.

   Don't – Speak fast or loud. You want to be heard and understood without being annoying.

8. **Do** – Make eye contact when speaking and answering questions. This shows you are being respectable, and is aware of what is going on in the interview.

   Don't –Interrupt or cut off the interviewer/s when questions are being asked. Listening is the key to answering the question correctly.

9. **Do** – Sit with perfect posture if possible. Hands should be on your lap or on the table in front of you over lapping each other.

   Don't – Talk with your hands or body. This makes you look aggressive or agitated during the interview and to the interviewer/s.

10. **Do** – Be well groomed from head to toe. Good hygiene means clean!
    - Men – should be clean shaved and hair neatly cut or trimmed.
    - Women – Make-up should be fresh looking, and hair should be neatly comb or styled.

    Don't – Come to an interview looking like you just got out of bed. Try not to wear strong smelling perfume or cologne as well. Also there should be no chewing gum, and eating of food or candy during the interview.

11. **Do** – Keep it small, neat, and simple if wearing jewelry.
    - Men – can wear a watch and/or bracelet.
    - Women – can wear stud earrings or small hoop style earrings, bracelet not bracelets (one will do), watch, and a simple necklace stopping at the neckline.

    Don't – Wear bulky or big jewelry or any body piercing (lip, tongue, eyebrow, nose, etc.). This can be distracting during an interview. You want the interviewer/s to focus on you, and not your jewelry. Also, do not expose your body art (tattoos). Again, you ALWAYS want to be professional.

12. **Do** – Send a "thank you" card or letter to each interviewer/s after your interview. It shows how appreciative you are of being interviewed. Example - *"I would like to thank you for allowing me the opportunity to interview for the IT Network Support position. It was a pleasure to meet with you, and I look forward to hearing from you soon."* Interviewer/s will read delivered mail before emails. They receive so many emails on a daily basis that your email could get lost in the shuffle, and be deleted.

    Don't - Call the interviewer/s everyday to see if you have the job. This can be taken as a form of harassment, and that is something you don't want. This can also ruin your chances of getting the job as well. Call a week after the interview date to show you are still interested in the position, and to get any feedback about your interview.

13. **Do** – Present your resume on professional resume paper. This indicates to the interviewer/s that you take yourself and what you do seriously. Plus it looks nice!

    Don't – Put your resume on color, copier or photo paper. This is not professional, and it will leave a bad impression with the interviewer/s. Also, NEVER add your photo (picture) to your resume. You do not want the employer to choose you because of your race, sex, religion, etc.; you want the employer to choose you based on your skills and ability to perform the job.

14. **Do** – Be polite and professional at all times. Give employers what they are looking for in future employees, and you will win them over every time.

Don't – Be rude or argumentative during an interview. It is unprofessional, and your interview will be cut short.

15. **Do** – Turn your cellular / mobile telephone completely off before, and during your interview. Always ask to use the company telephone to make a call if you need a ride after your interview is over. If you have a cellular / mobile telephone, and need to make a call, go into the company's lobby so you do not disturb the receptionist or front desk clerk.

Don't – Use the company phone without someone's permission, and do not answer a call or look at your cellular / mobile telephone during an interview. It is rude and distracting, and will be counted against you when the decision is made to bring on a new employee.

16. **Do** – Be truthful about your work history, and your experiences. The information you put on your resume, and application will be verified by the employer.

Don't – Be dishonest about yourself on your resume or application. Giving false or falsifying information on your resume, application, and in an interview will defiantly ruin your chances of getting the job.

17. **Do** – Ask questions. This will help you get a better understanding of the company, the job, salary expectation, etc., and you won't have to worry about any information not covered during the interview when the interview is over.

Don't – Ask personal information about the interviewer/s when asking questions. Keep the questions strictly business related!

FYI… Employers WOULD NEVER say anything negative to you about your appearance or your presentation during an interview. However, you will be JUDGED! When you present yourself in a way that is unprofessional from appearance to presentation it shows that you are not an expert in your field, and you have no desire or passion to do the job or represent their company.

V. Frequently Asked Questions

These are some of the questions asked by job seekers and career professionals, and the answers given by our consultants.

Q. Is presentation really important when it comes to you, and your resume?

A. Yes, very important. Presentation is the key to the door of success. Employers look at how a resume is presented to them, and will this person be a good fit within the company.

Q. Should your resume really be on resume paper?

A. Yes. Your resume represents you, and your experience. Putting your employment history on resume paper shows the employer you are professional, and you take yourself as well as what you do seriously.

Q. Should you always send a cover letter when applying for a job?

A. Yes. The cover letter informs the hiring manager or recruiter what position you are applying for or inquiring about.

Q. How many pages should a resume be?

A. In most cases two (2) pages depending on the years of experience you have. If you to have over six (6) years of experience then your resume should be at least three to four pages. (Only if you have the years of experience.).

Q. If I have over five (5) years of experience, should I put my experience on a one (1) page resume?

A. **No. One (1) page resumes are considered entry level. Job seekers with less then two (2) years of experience should use this style of resume. Experience, professional, and executive levels job seekers should never display their work history and skills on a one page resume.**

Q. Do employers look at resume's with more then two (2) pages?

A. **Yes, in some cases. However, the more you show your skills, and experience the more the employer will be interested. If employers are looking for job seekers with 5 or more years of experience along with the qualifications need for the job, a one or two page resume may not show it.**

Q. What is the difference between a Resume, and a Career Portfolio?

A. **A "Resume" gives a brief description of your job experiences, and a "Career Portfolio" gives a more detailed description of your work history.**

Q. What are some of the professional letters used, and when should they be used?

A. **Some of the professional letters used are the "Thank You", "Salary", and "Reference" letter. The "Thank You" letter should be used after an interview thanking each interviewer/s for the opportunity to interview with the company. The "Salary" letter should be used when an employer is inquiring about how much** money you are expecting to be paid. The "Reference" letter should be used when an employer is requesting names of former/current co-workers and/or supervisor/managers for verification of your work experience. The reference letter is also a good guide to use when filling in names of professional references on a job application too.

Q. Should you always send a "thank you" letter or card after every interview?

A. Yes. Always send a thank you letter or card to each of the interviewer/s even if you think the interview went or didn't go well.

Q. When should I use a professional resume writer? Why?

A. A professional resume writer should be used if you do not know how to create a professional resume or when you are not sure if your current resume is professional enough. Professional resume writers will know how to format your resume to showcase your skills, and talents as well as make your resume appealing to the eyes of employers.

Q. How important is it to find a job that you will like, and a company you can grow with?

A. It is very important. You want to find a job that is a match to your skills, so you can continue to do what you love and be successful at it. You want to work for a company that their employees career growth as well as encouragement to be successful.

Q. Can you lose out on an employment opportunity because of your appearance?

A. Yes. Employers will judge you from the time you arrive starting with the first person who sees you (the receptionist or greeter) to the time you interview, and when you leave the company after the interview. You want to *ALWAYS* look, and present yourself in a professional manner from the beginning to the end.

Q. Why should you arrive to an interview early?

A. Because you may have to fill out paperwork or take an employment test before the actual interview. Try to arrive at least 15 – 20 minutes early.

Remember….

- Research the company you wish to interview with or work for.

- Send a cover letter with your resume when applying for a job.

- Treat your resume like a fabulous dinner party.

- Be on time for your interview.

- Dress for success and wear a SUIT!

- Keep your appearance neat and simple.

- Be polite and respectable from the time you arrive to the time you leave.

- Be professional at all times.

- First impressions are lasting impressions.

- Know your work history, and the skills you have to perform the job.

- Presentation is the key that unlock many doors.

CONGRATULATIONS!!

You have just completed your first step to becoming a more successful you! Now you can go into an interview knowing how to play the game, and come out a "Winner!"

Notes

Notes

Notes

Notes

www.ingramcontent.com/pod-product-compliance
Lightning Source LLC
Chambersburg PA
CBHW021923170526
45157CB00005B/2165